Alcoholism

Look for these and other books in the Lucent
Overview series:

Alcoholism

by Arthur Diamond

LUCENT
B·O·O·K·S

FC BR
J
HV5066
.D53
1992

Library of Congress Cataloging-in-Publication Data

Diamond, Arthur
    Alcoholism / by Arthur Diamond.
        p.   cm. — (Lucent overview series)
    Includes bibliographical references and index.
    Summary: Discusses the causes and effects of alcohol abuse and describes some
of the measures used in the treatment and prevention of alcoholism.
    ISBN 1-56006-136-7 (acid-free paper)
    1. Alcoholism—Juvenile literature.   [1. Alcoholism.]
    I. Title.   II. Series.
    HV5066.D53   1992
    362.29'2—dc20   92-23601
                                                                            CIP
                                                                            AC

*To the men and women who worked beside me at
Max's Tavern, in Eugene, Oregon.*

Acknowledgments

The author would like to thank the following individuals who helped in the preparation of *Alcoholism*: Karen Likens, Dr. Rosalie Grossman, Lori Shein, Gary Rubin, and Karen Fitzgerald of the National Clearinghouse for Alcohol and Drug Information.

Contents

1

Alcoholism and Alcoholics

ALCOHOLISM IS DIFFERENT things to different people. Some experts call it a disorder, others a character flaw. A few consider it a state of mind. Today most experts believe that alcoholism can be defined in one of three ways: as a disease, as an addiction, or as voluntary behavior.

Whichever definition is used, professionals in medicine and counseling generally agree that alcoholism is a reliance or dependence on alcohol. Those who suffer from alcoholism can satisfy their need only by drinking more and more. When alcohol is unavailable alcoholics begin to experience nervousness, irritability, and physical discomfort; the longer they go without alcohol, the harsher their mental and physical discomforts become. For some alcoholics the need for alcohol becomes so great that they drink themselves to death.

Alcoholism is different from problem drinking in that problem drinkers "usually bring an end to their drinking when the problem is over," write Paul Dolmetsch and Gail Mauricette in their book *Teens Talk About Alcohol and Alcoholism*. "The alcoholic continues to drink on forever."

(Opposite page) Those who suffer from alcoholism have a reliance on alcohol. As this reliance grows, often, so does their drinking.

9

Most individuals and groups involved with the study and treatment of alcoholism, the American Medical Association among them, classify alcoholism as a disease. It is described this way because it has identifiable and progressive symptoms that, if untreated, lead to mental and physical damage and early death.

In many ways alcoholism is like any other disease. It is a disturbance of normal bodily function. It is often harmful or debilitating and can be fatal. It can be recognized or diagnosed by certain symptoms, and it can be treated. Like many other diseases, alcoholism is "diagnosable, treatable, progressive, and fatal . . . ," says writer Jack Mumey in *The Joy of Being Sober.*

Yet alcoholism is unlike other diseases in several ways. It is not contagious. It is not passed through the air like tuberculosis, nor through the intermingling of bodily fluids, like AIDS. One cannot get alcoholism like one gets a common cold. Some researchers believe that a tendency toward alcoholism can be physically passed on from parent to child, but this does not occur in every case.

Although family members do not "catch" the disease, they often suffer from its effects. The New York State Council on Alcoholism says that spouses and children of alcoholics are prone to "anxiety, depression, eating disorders, learning disabilities and a whole host of stress-related medical problems."

Addiction

Some people object to the characterization of alcoholism as a disease, however. That label, they suggest, implies that some powerful, overwhelming force has taken over the body, leaving the alcoholic helpless in the face of his or her predicament. A disease often is beyond the control of the individual who suffers from it. People who have cancer or AIDS, for example, cannot will it away or change their behavior to make the disease disappear. Alcoholic individuals, on the other hand, can control their disease by not drinking.

Some researchers prefer to characterize alcoholism as an addiction. This is because an addiction is essentially a psychological and physical dependence that can be overcome through individual effort.

Psychological dependence is more or less an unconscious behavior. It usually begins with some anxiety or specific problem—like difficulties with schoolwork or discomfort with a boss. The individual repeatedly turns to some experience—say, cigarette smoking or the drinking of alcohol—to feel better. The physical sensation of smoke drawing through the lungs or of alcohol deadening the senses becomes an experience during which the individual turns away from difficulties. When faced with a problem, the individual always knows where to seek a sense of escape and satisfaction. Physical dependence occurs as the body needs more and more of a substance to function normally. Together these psychological and physical dependencies may be difficult to conquer, but many people have done so successfully.

Some people turn to alcohol as a means of coping with anxiety and stress.

Voluntary behavior

Finally, some feel that alcoholism is more or less a voluntary behavior rather than a disease over which an individual has no control. Herbert Fingarette, a philosophy professor at the University of California at Santa Barbara, believes that individuals have much control over their drinking. He argues in his book *Heavy Drinking: The Myth of Alcoholism as a Disease* that the idea of alcoholism as a disease implies a loss of control. To the contrary, Fingarette says, "alcoholics can

Alcohol can provide a temporary sense of relief from problems, but it does not do anything to solve those problems.

and do have a great deal of control over their drinking."

Fingarette disputes the idea that alcoholism is a disease passed from parents to children. To support his argument Fingarette cites several studies on children of adoptive and biological alcoholic parents. In one study, done by Dr. Robert Cloninger, a professor of psychiatry at Washington University in St. Louis, Missouri, researchers found that peer pressure or a family's attitude toward drinking could dramatically affect a person's interaction with alcohol. This proved to be the case even among a population considered at high risk for developing alcoholism—children of alcoholics.

Who is an alcoholic?

Although experts disagree on a precise definition for alcoholism, most agree that all alcoholics have two things in common: they drink alcohol, and alcohol influences their behavior, often disrupting personal, professional, and family life.

Dr. Donald W. Goodwin, in his book *Is Alcoholism Hereditary?*, offers an apt description of an alcoholic: "An alcoholic is a person who drinks, has problems from drinking, but goes on drinking anyway."

An alcoholic is not always easily recognized. Some alcoholics manage to hide their drinking from friends and family—sometimes for years. "They don't tell people when they are drunk, or they try to act cool about it when they are," write Dolmetsch and Mauricette. Some alcoholics learn to cover up a drinking problem by hiding liquor bottles in a locked drawer at the office or in secret places in the home. Many alcoholics learn how to function in public even when they are under the influence of alcohol. This often means that their problem goes unnoticed.

Differences among alcoholics

Alcoholism is not characterized by any single drinking pattern, either. Some alcoholics, dubbed "weekend alcoholics," can go without drinking for several days or even weeks at a time. Others drink daily or even hourly.

Despite these differences most experts generally agree that alcoholics can be divided into two groups. One group includes those who are physically addicted to or dependent upon alcohol. The other group includes those who drink to extremes but have no physical addiction to alcohol.

The latter group often drinks in response to immediate personal, family, and work-related problems. Alcohol provides them with a way of escaping or forgetting what bothers them. People in this group may show signs of declining health and impaired social functions, like difficulties performing at work or communicating at home, as a result of their drinking. Once the problem that prompted the drinking is solved, however,

Reprinted with special permission of King Feature Syndicate, Inc.

these people often stop drinking.

People who are physically addicted to alcohol also drink to extremes. Unlike the other group, however, these people continue to drink even after their immediate problems have been solved. In a sense, alcohol helps these drinkers maintain a certain level of functioning. Eventually the alcoholic develops a tolerance to alcohol, meaning that it takes more alcohol to obtain the same effect. Alcoholism researcher Sandie Johnson explains that this physical dependence is "often felt in craving and in the development of tolerance."

While some experts contend that alcohol abusers are not suffering from alcoholism, other experts state that both kinds of drinkers can be said to be suffering from alcoholism. Says Johnson: "The trend is toward defining alcoholism by what it does to you rather than in terms of how much you drink."

For this reason, a person who consumes alcohol every day is not necessarily an alcoholic. Most drinkers, in fact, are social drinkers. Social drinking does not have an exact definition, for it is difficult to say how many drinks a person can consume and still remain "sociable." But it can be said that a person is a social drinker rather than an alcoholic if drinking does not prove to be a problem.

In other words, a social drinker is not compulsive about alcohol and does not have some deep-seated need to drink. One young alcoholic quoted by Dolmetsch and Mauricette says that most alcoholics "have compulsive personalities . . . if one beer tastes good, then two have got to taste better."

Alcoholism is widespread

While social drinkers predominate, alcoholism is widespread in the United States. It is a leading cause of death, behind cancer and heart disease. About fifteen million, or 3 percent, of American adults experience problems at home and on the job that are related directly to alcohol consumption, according to the 1990 *Seventh Special Report to the U.S. Congress on Alcohol and Health.* About nine million of those are physically dependent on alcohol, while another six million drink to extremes without experiencing addiction. Additionally, at least forty million people suffer from the destructive behavior of an alcoholic relative. "It is no exaggeration to call alcoholism a social plague," James E. Payne and Dr. Kenneth Blum write in *Alcohol and the Addictive Brain.*

In the general population, social drinkers probably outnumber alcoholics. A social drinker is one who does not develop a need for alcohol.

Alcoholism reaches deep into the mosaic that is American society. It affects people of all races and ethnic backgrounds, both sexes, all ages, and all economic levels. About seventy-six million Americans, or 43 percent of the adult population, have been exposed to alcoholism in the family at some point in their lives, a 1991 federal survey found. The survey, conducted by the National Center for Health Statistics and the National Clearinghouse for Alcohol and Drug Information, also noted that 10 percent of adults have been married to or had a marriage-like relationship with an alcoholic or problem drinker.

Alcoholism research focusing on race and ethnicity has only begun in recent years. However, the National Clearinghouse for Alcohol Information has reported that approximately 22 percent

Not all drinkers become alcoholics, but studies show that at least 5 percent of heavy drinkers will eventually battle alcoholism.

of white men and 19 percent of black men are heavy drinkers. The National Clearinghouse also has reported that 11 percent of black women and 4 percent of white women are heavy drinkers. While not all heavy drinkers are alcoholics, at least 5 percent of heavy drinkers become alcoholics, according to the American Council on Science and Health.

Underage drinking

Nor are there age barriers to alcoholism. Children as young as seven have been diagnosed as alcoholics and one out of ten people over age sixty has an alcohol problem. While underage drinking has dropped 20 percent since 1988, statistics released by the federal government in January 1992 reveal that alcohol is still the most abused substance among youth under age twenty-one. Thirty percent of high school seniors surveyed in 1991 reported heavy drinking (five or more drinks in a row) at least once in the two weeks prior to the survey.

Alcoholism affects rich and poor; it affects people who are highly educated and people who are less educated. In Atlanta, Georgia, for example, certain professional groups have formed their own Alcoholics Anonymous chapters. Alcoholic attorneys meet in a chapter called the "Legal Eagles," alcoholic pilots meet in a chapter called "Birds of a Feather," and alcoholic ministers gather in a chapter called the "Drunk Monks."

Alcoholism seems to be more prevalent in some groups of people than others. Men, for example, usually outnumber women in alcoholism studies. One recently completed twenty-year study by the Berkeley Alcohol Research Group found that as many as 30 percent of American men have had some kind of drinking problem.

However, women have been the subject of

fewer alcoholism studies and this may account for the perception that alcoholism is more common among men than women. The studies that have been done suggest that about 2 percent of all American women are alcoholics. This figure may be on the rise: a 1988 study revealed that the percentage of women arrested for drunk driving increased year to year over a period of five years.

Studies have also found that native Americans suffer from alcoholism in high numbers. A 1989 report in the *Journal of Studies on Alcohol* concluded that alcoholism among native Americans has "reached epidemic proportions and has been described as the number one health problem in these cultural groups."

The prevalence of alcoholism in native American communities can be seen in several areas. Alcohol is associated with three-fourths of all traumatic deaths among native Americans. Cirrhosis of the liver, a disease often caused by too much alcohol drinking, kills native Americans at a rate three times that of other Americans. In addition, fetal alcohol syndrome, a disorder in which a fetus is poisoned by alcohol in the mother's bloodstream, appears at a rate thirty-three times higher than in white Americans.

Around the world

Alcoholism is not limited to the United States, of course. It afflicts people in many parts of the world. Public health researchers in Mexico, Hungary, Finland, Italy, and South Korea have reported problems with alcoholism in their general populations.

The former Soviet Union, for example, has long had a problem with alcoholism. In Russia today, alcoholism continues to be a problem. "Drinking has gripped the Russian character like a python," author Boyd Gibbons writes in the

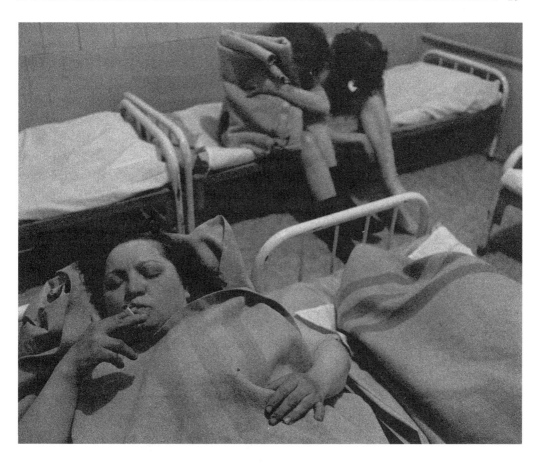

Three women sober up in a Russian holding cell. Russian police use cells such as this for intoxicated individuals.

February 1992 issue of *National Geographic*. Just as Americans drink alcohol for many reasons, Russians also drink for different reasons. However, in trying to characterize the Russian affection for alcohol, one Russian citizen explained: "Our national tradition is to drink for any reason, or for no reason."

Accurate statistics are hard to come by. But a leading Moscow researcher, Dr. Boris Segal, reported in 1990 that more than 17 percent of Soviet citizens aged twenty-one and older suffered from alcoholism in 1985. This number, if correct, is more than five times the number of alcoholics in the United States.

Alcoholism, and problems related to it, have

been documented in many countries. France, known for its wine, has a high incidence of alcohol-related problems. It has twice the death rate by cirrhosis of the liver as in the United States. Great Britain, too, has problems with alcoholism, although most alcoholics in Britain are beer drinkers. In Finland public drunkenness is widespread, although drunk driving and alcohol-related traffic deaths are rare compared with the United States, where nearly half the forty-five thousand annual highway deaths are alcohol related. Over the last thirty years deaths from liver cirrhosis have risen more than fivefold in Hungary. During the same three decades South Korea has seen an explosion in heavy drinking. South Koreans now consume more alcohol per capita than does any other nation. Italy, like France, has a long history of wine making and wine drinking. About

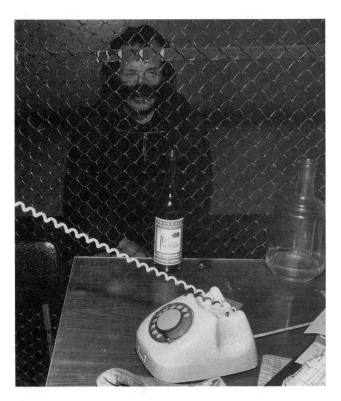

A drunk Moscow resident awaits transport to a city holding cell where he will be held until he sobers up.

twenty thousand Italians die annually from cirrhosis of the liver, and authorities there estimate that about 9 percent of the population are alcoholics.

Perhaps the most telling statistic of all comes from Alcoholics Anonymous, a well-known organization that runs alcoholism recovery programs worldwide. Alcoholics Anonymous claims it has two million participants in 136 countries. Together, these statistics indicate that alcoholism is a problem of worldwide proportions.

Frenchmen drink wine at a local bistro. France, known for its exceptional wines, has a high rate of alcoholism.

2

The Causes of Alcoholism

UNTIL THE TWENTIETH century alcoholism was generally thought to be caused by moral weakness or wickedness of character. Alcoholics were thought to have done something bad in their lives to deserve their fate and were shunned by society. The drink and the drinker were basically thought to be evil.

Research—especially studies conducted over the past twenty years—has convinced most people that this is not the case. Alcoholism is now widely viewed as having three possible causes. Genetics, or the biological processes through which parents pass certain characteristics on to their children, is believed to play a part in causing alcoholism. Environment, or the surroundings and influences that make up an individual's home and neighborhood, is also thought to contribute to alcoholism. Psychological factors, including how a person deals with stressful situations, may also contribute to alcoholism.

(Opposite page) Psychological factors, such as stress, may contribute to alcoholism. Individuals with a history of alcoholism in their families may be especially vulnerable.

Much of the current research on the causes of alcoholism focuses on these three areas. Researchers are trying to learn if one of these areas plays a dominant role in causing alcoholism or if alcoholism results from some combination of genetics, environment, and psychology.

Narrowing the field to a single cause is a difficult—perhaps impossible—task. Even trained researchers cannot easily determine which factors influence a person's behavior. Chromosomes, which carry the genetic information that determines traits such as hair and eye color, might bear some responsibility, while environment and psychological factors might also have some influence. "The influences of homes and chromosomes on the final product—the person—quickly become virtually inseparable," writes Dr. Donald Goodwin.

Alcoholism runs in families

What scientists have discovered, however, is that alcoholism tends to run in families. This means that it is likely that a person who suffers from alcoholism had parents, and probably even grandparents, who were alcoholics. "The strongest predictor of future alcoholism," says Goodwin, "is a family history of alcoholism."

This does not mean that the son or daughter of an alcoholic will absolutely become an alcoholic too. Rather, it means that the sons and daughters of alcoholic parents are more likely to become alcoholics than are people from families untouched by alcoholism. "Sons of alcoholic fathers are at four times greater risk of alcoholism than others," the Children of Alcoholics Foundation concludes. "Daughters of alcoholic mothers are three times more likely to become future alcoholics than others. . . ."

Researchers have spent a great deal of time studying this family connection. So far they have determined two possible links between alcoholism and families. One link appears to be biological or genetic. The other appears to be influenced by environment.

Scientists are conducting studies to learn whether alcoholism is passed genetically from parents to children. Some early research, including a 1973 study in Denmark, strongly suggests that this is the case. In that study researchers found that young men who had alcoholic fathers but were adopted and raised by nonalcoholic parents had a relatively high rate of alcoholism. These young men were three times as likely to develop alcoholism as were youths born to nonalcoholic parents. Although these young men had no contact with the alcoholic birth parent and lived in environments in which alcoholism was not present, many still became alcoholics. This and later research seem to support the theory that alcoholism has some sort of genetic link.

Research into this link has taken different directions. Some research centers on efforts to find out if there is an actual gene for alcoholism.

Researchers now know that alcoholism tends to run in families.

Genes contain the information that specifies which characteristics are passed from parents to offspring. Genes determine hair and eye color, for example. Researchers also know that some diseases are passed on through the genes. Some researchers wonder whether alcoholism is also passed in this way from parents to children. "What the researchers eventually want is to identify the influential genes," writes Boyd Gibbons of *National Geographic*.

Some researchers believe that a gene for alcoholism will directly affect the brain's internal chemistry. It may contribute to some kind of deficiency or imbalance that leads to a craving for alcohol. It may also cause craving for substances besides alcohol. Authors Kenneth Blum and James Payne point to a study of recovering male alcoholics and their sons. The study found that the groups had similar neurological imbalances and deficiencies. It also concluded that the sons of the alcoholics were, at an early age, "at serious

risk of developing cravings not only for alcohol, but for other addictive drugs such as nicotine and marijuana, also like their fathers."

Other studies have focused on the brain. Some researchers think brain waves or patterns of human brain activity might provide biological markers, or clues, about who is prone to becoming an alcoholic. In the mid-1980s Dr. Henri Begleiter, a neuroscientist in the College of Medicine at State University of New York, identified a brain-wave marker in sons of alcoholics.

Genetic predisposition

So far, however, most evidence suggests that the genetic connection to alcoholism might be much less direct. Rather than being determined by a specific gene or brain wave, alcoholism might be influenced by a genetic predisposition. Predisposition is an inclination toward some behavior, such as child's tendency to follow a parent's vocation, or a tree's inclination to grow toward the sun. Genetic predisposition means that while there may be a family history of alcoholism, and possibly a biological cause, family members will not automatically become alcoholics. Determination and willpower may prevent the development of alcoholism.

Experts point out that predisposition does not mean predestination, or that a person is fated or destined to be an alcoholic. Dr. Begleiter explains the difference between predestination and predisposition:

> Alcoholism is different from Huntington's chorea, a directly inherited disease caused by a single gene—you have the gene, you get Huntington's. What you inherit in alcoholism is not a disease, it's a predisposition. . . . You probably inherit some genes, each with small effect, that make you susceptible not only to alcoholism but also to a number of dysfunctional [impaired] behaviors influenced by your environment.

Environment, some researchers believe, plays a role equal to, or maybe greater than, genetics in the development of alcoholism. Several recent studies support this theory. A 1992 study, conducted by University of Minnesota psychologist Matt McGue, found that environmental factors outweigh genetic factors in men and women alcoholics.

Other studies raise additional questions about genetics and environment as causes of alcoholism. A University of Michigan study published in 1990 surveyed hundreds of offspring of men with drinking problems. The study found that nearly two-thirds of the offspring drank very little or not at all. In 1989 a group of researchers in Philadelphia surveyed eighty-three male college students. The researchers found no differences in the amount or frequency of drinking between the sons of alcoholics and the sons of non-alcoholics.

Studies such as these seem to indicate that something other than, or in addition to, genetics determines who will and will not become an alcoholic. That other factor may be environment. Author Alfie Kohn writes that "even researchers who insist that genes do play a role generally add that drinking is profoundly affected by one's social and family environment, and the choices one makes. . . ."

Learning by watching

Psychological factors, too, are thought to be an influence. For instance, a person at risk for developing alcoholism may enter adulthood with no alcohol-related problems. Yet some sudden diffi-

The home environment may contribute as much to alcoholism as does genetic predisposition.

Children learn a lot about acceptable behavior by watching and imitating their parents.

culty, perhaps related to marriage or work, might put so much pressure on that person that he or she begins drinking heavily. Because this person has a genetic predisposition to alcoholism, the likelihood of developing alcoholism is fairly high.

Researchers also know that children learn many ways of behaving by watching and imitating their parents. Some suspect that this, too, may play a part in alcoholism. According to Dr. Goodwin, "Parental attitudes toward drinking surely influence the drinking behavior of their children, although it is difficult to say what attitudes produce what behaviors."

However, many children of alcoholics do not become alcoholics themselves. Some develop a deep dislike of, or aversion to, alcohol after seeing what it has done to their parents or other family members.

There is still much research to be done and many questions to be answered concerning the causes of alcoholism. While no one yet knows any exact single cause for alcoholism, experts have strong evidence that alcoholism has its roots in genetic, environmental, and psychological factors. They also know that alcoholism tends to run in families. Many questions ultimately involve the idea of a combination of factors working together to produce alcoholism in the individual.

3

The Physical Effects of Alcoholism

ALCOHOLISM AFFECTS DIFFERENT people in different ways. Most research suggests, however, that alcoholism—that is, a long-term and extreme reliance on alcohol—has dire consequences for the human body. Alcoholism can, and frequently does, result in damage to essential body organs, from the brain to the heart to the liver. A 1990 report to Congress noted that "virtually no part of the body is spared the effects of excessive alcohol consumption."

The physical effects of alcoholism can even extend beyond the alcoholic. A pregnant woman who drinks heavily can literally poison the fetus growing inside of her.

Yet all alcoholics do not suffer the same physical consequences of their alcoholism. An individual's size and internal body chemistry, as well as how much and how frequently a person drinks, determine alcoholism's physical effects.

"Incredibly, a person may consume a ferocious quantity of alcohol, maybe a fifth or a quart of whiskey a day for twenty years or longer, and when he dies a 'natural' death, his brain, liver,

(Opposite page) A motorist undergoes a sobriety test given by a police officer. Alcohol slows reflexes, diminishes judgment, and affects motor skills.

33

pancreas, and coronary arteries appear normal," Dr. Donald Goodwin writes.

The varied effects of drinking alcohol can also be seen in people who are not alcoholics. One person, for example, might experience a drunken feeling after only one drink while another person can consume three drinks with little effect.

While the effects vary, however, the route alcohol takes through the body is generally the same. Although alcohol is often thought to be a stimulant because it is used in many social occasions, it is, in fact, a depressant. Alcohol slows the functioning of the central nervous system and the brain. Reflexes are dulled and judgment dimin-

Alcohol irritates the tissues of the mouth and esophagus (a) as it enters the body. The alcohol then passes to the stomach (b) where some alcohol is immediately absorbed into the bloodstream. The remaining alcohol travels to the small intestine (c) where it is absorbed into the bloodstream and carried to the heart (d). The heart pumps the blood—and whatever alcohol it has absorbed—to other parts of the body including the brain (e). From the brain the alcohol is pumped to the liver (f). The liver processes what it can for energy and the rest is expelled from the body.

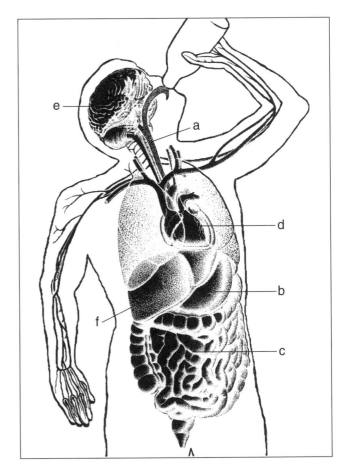

ished. Drinking too much can result in passing out or even death; for every individual, there is a lethal dose of alcohol, generally related to body size.

Irritation

The physiological effects of alcohol begin with ingestion. With even a small sip of alcohol, the tissues of the drinker's mouth and esophagus become both irritated and numbed.

After being swallowed the alcohol passes to the stomach. Here, about 20 percent of the alcohol in the drink is absorbed into the bloodstream. The remaining alcohol irritates the stomach lining, causing the secretion of gastric juices, which normally aid in the digestion of food; these juices, set loose in an empty stomach, further irritate the stomach. In some people prolonged use of alcohol on an empty stomach may lead to inflammation of the stomach lining and peptic ulcers, which are holes caused by the digestive juices.

From the stomach the alcohol travels to the small intestine, which serves as a passageway from the stomach to the anus. In the intestine alcohol can destroy enzymes, which are the proteins that keep the body functioning. From the small intestine the remaining alcohol is absorbed into the bloodstream. About 5 percent of the alcohol leaves the body through urine, sweat, or exhaled breath.

Alcohol that reaches the bloodstream is carried directly to the heart. As a result the heart increases its rate of beating and blood pressure rises. Large amounts of alcohol—in excess of three drinks a day—can cause hypertension, or sustained high blood pressure. Blood pressure does not return to normal levels until a week after a person stops drinking. The heart pumps the alcohol through the bloodstream to other parts of the body, including the brain.

The brain is affected as the alcohol reaches its surface. Nerve centers governing speech are numbed, and motor skills—like driving or operating heavy machinery—are impaired. Also, vision, speech, and judgment are all impeded. A great quantity of alcohol will cause the drinker to pass out; this is believed to be a self-preserving action by the brain, to keep more alcohol from being consumed. The parts of the brain that control breathing can be affected by too much alcohol, and the drinker can actually suffocate from respiratory failure.

Alcohol in the brain also causes the blood vessels to expand. This expansion causes the swollen blood vessels to press against the skull, and usually a headache results. Many drinkers experience this unpleasant sensation, known as a hangover, the morning after a night of drinking. The blood vessels eventually return to normal size a few hours later and the headache disappears.

From the brain the alcohol is pumped through the bloodstream to the liver. In the liver special enzymes—proteins that help produce chemical reactions throughout the body—go to work on the ethanol, the active component of alcohol. These enzymes trigger the conversion of the ethanol into carbon dioxide, water, and energy. This process, called oxidation, occurs at the rate of one-third of an ounce per hour. The liver retains the ethanol's harmful toxins, or poisons, while the rest of it—now broken up into other components—is excreted from the body.

Physical dependence

Unlike a social drinker, who can take a drink without feeling a need for more, an alcoholic develops a physical dependence on alcohol. This means that the alcoholic's body comes to need the alcohol to function normally. The body's

growing dependence on alcohol is most apparent when an alcoholic tries to stop drinking.

Many alcoholics who give up alcohol initially experience anxiety, sleeplessness, shaking, and hallucinations. The severity of these problems depends on how much and how long the alcoholic has been drinking.

As a rule alcohol withdrawal usually lasts two to seven days. The alcoholic gets "the shakes" a few hours after having stopped drinking. Dr. Goodwin describes this occurrence: "[The alcoholic's] eyelids flutter, his tongue quivers, but, most conspicuously, his hands shake, so that transporting a cup of coffee from saucer to mouth is a major undertaking."

After a day or two of abstinence the alcoholic might begin hallucinating—seeing and hearing things that are not there. These hallucinations can be frightening and may seem as real as life to the individual. In Janet Grosshandler's *Coping with*

Too much alcohol can cause a drinker to pass out. This may be the brain's way of keeping an individual from drinking more alcohol.

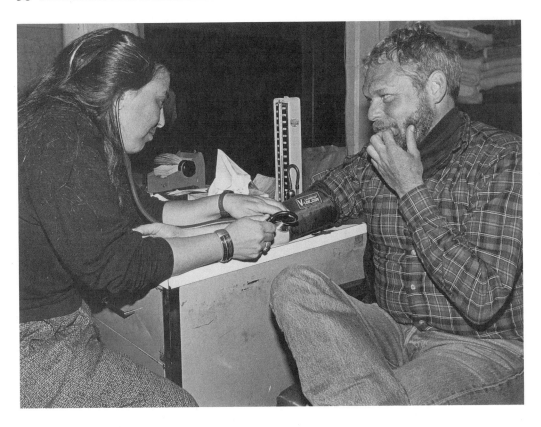

A nurse checks the blood pressure of a man who is an alcoholic. High blood pressure is common among alcoholics. It usually does not return to normal until after a person stops drinking.

Alcohol Abuse, one former alcoholic described a feeling of "bugs moving all over my skin, inside and out, and I couldn't get them off no matter how hard I tried. I thought I was going crazy."

The shakes

Hallucinations like these are usually part of the condition known as delirium tremens, or "the DTs." Delirium tremens is an altered state of reality in which a person is hardly aware of the immediate environment. This person may suffer from loss of memory, sleeplessness, agitation, and hallucinations.

The DTs are considered a medical emergency demanding immediate hospitalization. The patient can also experience high fever and dehydration. Author Ross Fishman, in his book *Alcohol and*

Alcoholism, reports that "if untreated, the DTs are fatal in as many as 20 percent of the cases."

The liver

Alcohol drinking in the quantity and frequency practiced by many people who suffer from alcoholism can have other effects. Over a period of time involving heavy alcohol consumption, the liver is prone to disease and outright failure. The liver acts as the body's filter. Alcohol in the liver prevents the important breakdown of fats that accumulate within liver cells. The fatty cells can rupture or develop into cysts. These fatty cells or cysts then replace normal, healthy cells.

After years of drinking these cysts usually grow. They turn into bulky, fibrous tissue in the liver, slowing down the normal flow of blood through the organ. Because of this fibrous scar tissue, or cirrhosis, the liver, which is starved for blood, may fail. Liver failure can cause sudden death.

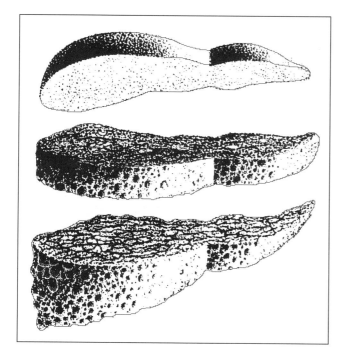

Alcohol can cause a healthy liver (top) to develop fatty cells or cysts (center). The fibrous scar tissue (bottom), or cirrhosis, that results from the growth of cysts or fatty cells can cause liver failure and death.

40

A healthy brain (top) is compared to a brain with tissue deterioration and cell loss hastened by heavy drinking (bottom).

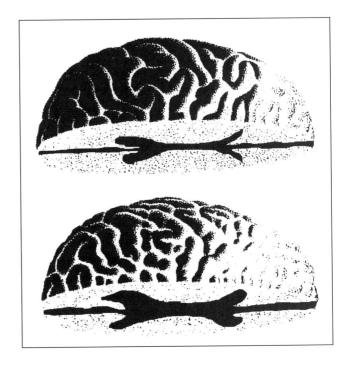

It is uncertain how much alcohol over how long a period of time needs to be consumed for the liver to become impaired. A 1990 report to Congress cites evidence from studies showing that fat accumulation and other structural changes in the liver could be induced in young, nonalcoholic volunteers in about a week of drinking alcohol. The amount of alcohol given to the volunteers was not great—it was, in fact, small enough so that it did not induce intoxication in any individual.

The pancreas and stomach

Alcohol can affect other organs besides the liver. The pancreas is a soft, irregularly shaped organ at the back wall of the upper abdomen. It produces important hormones, including insulin, and discharges enzymes into the bloodstream. The pancreas is especially vulnerable to alcohol abuse. In his 1987 book, *The Treatment of Alco-*

holism, Dr. Edgar P. Nace reveals that studies in the United States have shown that pancreatitis, an inflammation that can severely impair the pancreas, "is caused in one out of three instances by alcohol."

The stomach, too, can be affected by long-term alcohol abuse. The stomach lining is coated by a protective mucus that can become irritated and eaten away by alcohol. This process may continue until small holes, or ulcers, appear in the lining.

Alcoholism also produces gastritis, which is an inflammation of the stomach. According to Dr. Nace, a 1981 study reported that an advanced stage of gastritis that involves bleeding in the stomach "is five times more common in the alcoholic population."

The brain

Alcoholism can also damage the brain. This damage can result in poor vision, loss of coordination, memory loss, and loss of sensation. Heavy alcohol use over a long period of time damages the brain by killing brain cells. The human brain has many more cells than it needs, so some loss—possibly 10 percent—is not especially serious.

But with long-term alcohol use 20 or 30 percent of the brain cells are destroyed. Memory and thinking processes are impaired. Medical examinations conducted just after death dramatically demonstrate the deterioration process that occurs with long-term alcohol abuse. Examinations of the brains of longtime alcoholics show signs of general tissue deterioration as well as specific cell loss in at least two areas of the brain associated with memory functions.

Some studies associate alcoholism with increased risk for various types of cancers, includ-

The risk of developing cancer increases when excessive alcohol consumption and smoking are combined.

ing cancers of the liver, esophagus, and larynx. While alcohol does not appear to be a carcinogen, or direct cause of cancer, it may weaken enzymes that attack and repel carcinogens. Cigarette smoke, for example, is a carcinogen that passes through the larynx and esophagus of a smoker. Weakened enzymes in these organs could be a problem. A recent study found that the combination of daily alcohol consumption and smoking twenty-five cigarettes a day made the risk of getting cancer of the esophagus much higher than did either habit by itself.

Poisoning the fetus

Whatever the physical effects of alcoholism, usually it is the alcoholic alone who experiences them. Not so in the case of fetal alcohol syndrome (FAS), a disorder that reaches inside the womb and lives on in the child long after birth. Any woman who drinks heavily during pregnancy runs the risk of bearing a child who suffers from fetal alcohol syndrome.

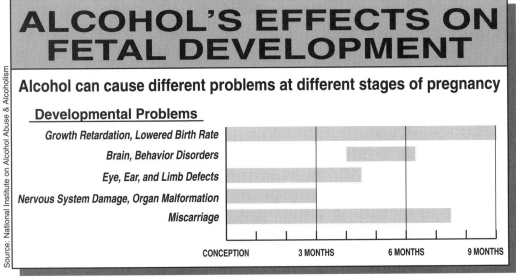

ALCOHOL'S EFFECTS ON FETAL DEVELOPMENT

Alcohol can cause different problems at different stages of pregnancy

Developmental Problems

Growth Retardation, Lowered Birth Rate
Brain, Behavior Disorders
Eye, Ear, and Limb Defects
Nervous System Damage, Organ Malformation
Miscarriage

CONCEPTION   3 MONTHS   6 MONTHS   9 MONTHS

Source: National Institute on Alcohol Abuse & Alcoholism

In a pregnant woman alcohol is taken by the blood to the uterus and absorbed through the placenta, which is the nourishing and protective wall around the fetus. Inside the placenta the alcohol comes into direct contact with the fetus. Fetal exposure to the alcohol can cause a variety of problems, including loss of vision, hearing, and mental ability. FAS is a leading cause of mental retardation. Some of these problems are caused by alcohol's reduction of the flow of oxygen to the brain.

Many families in the United States have had experience with fetal alcohol syndrome. Author E. L. Abel writes that among alcohol-dependent women in the United States, approximately 25 out of 1,000 births may result in a baby with FAS. The Children of Alcoholics Foundation estimates that 3,700 to 7,400 FAS babies are born annually in the United States.

FAS babies typically weigh less than other babies at birth. They also frequently suffer from heart murmurs, mental retardation, and urinary tract problems. Many also have an abnormally small head, short nose, thin upper lip, indistinct groove between upper lip and nose, small wide-set eyes, and flat cheeks.

Malcolm O'Donovan* is a fairly typical FAS child. His mother, George Steinmetz writes in the February 1992 issue of *National Geographic*, was an alcoholic who had been drinking a bottle of vodka a day before she learned that she was two months pregnant. Malcolm, Steinmetz writes, was

> undersized at birth, with kidneys and a stomach that didn't work properly; he had to be tube-fed until he was 14 months old. . . . His head is smaller than normal, and he also has facial abnormalities typical of FAS children—small wide-set

*Author's Note: Malcolm O'Donovan is not the child's real name.

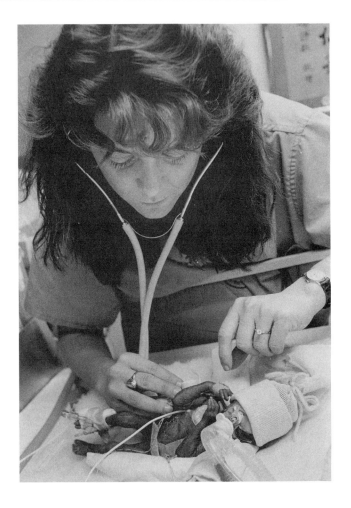

eyes, a thin upper lip, a short upturned nose, and a receding chin. He was born with damaged corneas, and his eyelids drooped.

Studies indicate that children born with FAS are likely to have difficulties concentrating in school. A 1986 study done in Seattle, Washington, by researcher A. P. Streissguth found that children of women who drank at least one ounce of alcohol daily during pregnancy tended to be easily distracted and slow to respond to instructions. In one part of the test, for example, these children did not respond as quickly as other children to orders from the computer to press certain buttons. Other parts of the test included measuring the ability of the children to respond while being distracted by noisy clicks from the computer. Again the children of women who drank daily during pregnancy had slower responses than others.

Studies show that heavy drinking during pregnancy does not guarantee the birth of a baby with FAS. The drinking mother's genetic structure seems to play a role in determing whether her children will develop FAS. Sometimes, in twins, one will be born with FAS, while the other will be born without it.

However, author Steinmetz reports, some experts believe that any amount of alcohol consumption during pregnancy puts the unborn child at risk. Nearly all doctors believe that heavy drinking in the first twelve weeks of pregnancy can be dangerous because this is one of the most important stages in fetal development.

4

The Effects of Alcoholism on Society

ALCOHOLISM HAS MANY serious and damaging effects on society. It can destroy families, cost millions in the workplace, and can lead to suicide or accidental death.

Alcoholics themselves are not the sole victims of alcoholism: it is a disease of individuals, families, and society. According to Al-Anon Family Groups, "every alcoholic deeply affects at least four or five others, i.e., spouse, parent, child, friend, co-worker." Author Ross Fishman puts it this way: "Nearly 20 percent of the entire population of the United States suffers from the ravages of alcoholism."

Alcoholism puts many pressures on a family. Financial security may be one concern, because an alcoholic parent may be unable to hold onto a job. Alcoholism can also put a great deal of stress on the marital relationship and on the children of the alcoholic.

Although the causes of alcoholism are better understood today, alcoholics are still sometimes viewed as lacking in control and moral character. This view perpetuates the stigma, or shame, at-

(Opposite page) One of the most obvious and tragic effects of alcohol abuse is the death toll from auto accidents caused by people driving drunk.

tached to being an alcoholic. The stigma of alcoholism as well as the daily reality of living with an alcoholic touches all family members.

In Eric Ryerson's book *When Your Parents Drink Too Much*, one girl relates the experience of living with an alcoholic parent:

> On the outside, everything looks nice and normal with our family. We live in a nice house and a nice neighborhood. But that's just appearances, because inside what's going on is crazy. Lots of drinking, fighting, craziness. You can't let anybody know what it's really like.

The constant emotional, and sometimes physical, battering experienced by the families of alcoholics breeds low self-esteem and conflicting emotions. Spouses of alcoholics often try to excuse the behavior of the alcoholic while at the same time denying that a problem even exists. Denial is a common problem for both the alcoholic and the spouse. It is difficult to solve a problem if one does not acknowledge that the problem even exists. With help a marriage can survive alco-

Outward appearances can be misleading. Families ravaged by alcoholism sometimes appear to lead perfectly normal lives.

A twenty-two-year-old man who was neglected as a child by an alcoholic parent uses art to recall moments and feelings from that time.

holism—but many do not. One study estimated that 40 percent of the nation's alcoholics have been in marriages that ended in divorce.

Troubled children

Children of alcoholics also experience difficulties related to having an alcoholic parent. The Children of Alcoholics Foundation estimates that there are 28 million children of alcoholics in this country and that 7 million of them are under the age of eighteen. One out of every eight Americans, the foundation says, is the child of an alcoholic.

One of the biggest problems facing children of alcoholics is that the alcoholic parent, consumed

A thirteen-year-old boy's drawing of life with an alcoholic father. The boy's prayerful plea expresses the pain felt by many children of alcoholics.

by alcoholism, is essentially an absent parent. "As far as family relationships, even if the parents are physically present, functioning and working, they are absent. Their primary relationship is with their chemical. Others are just helping or hindering this relationship," says Karen Likens, a substance abuse counselor and family therapist in Portland, Oregon.

There are specific problems, too, that plague children of alcoholics. They may experience headaches, bedwetting, and nightmares. Physical problems such as these are thought to be a result of the tremendous strain of living with an alcoholic parent.

The Children of Alcoholics Foundation reports:

> As youngsters, children of alcoholics may have . . . headaches, tiredness and stomachaches, although no specific illnesses are detected. Also, they may

have tics, nausea, bedwetting, sleep problems, asthma and sensory problems with noise, bright lights, heat and cold more often than other children. . . . [They may also] evidence such problems as emotional detachment, dependency, aggression, confusion of personal identify and lower self-esteem.

Some experts believe that one problem—nightmares—is caused by a fear of physical violence. Children of alcoholics, Dolmetsch and Mauricette write, "can be so scared of alcoholic parents beating the tar out of them that they wake up in a cold sweat, having dreamed that it happened."

These young people often develop problems or suffer injuries that require visits to the hospital. Drug addiction and eating disorders, for example, are common problems experienced by children of alcoholics. The Children of Alcoholics Foundation reports that these young people

> have higher rates of in-patient hospital admissions, spend more days in hospitals, incur greater hospital charges and are more susceptible to specific illness than other children. Their major health problems are substance abuse, mental disorders, injuries, and poisonings.

The painful home situation caused by alcoholism leads some young people to withdraw from schoolwork and friends.

These types of problems can be a cause of poor performance at school, too. As Ryerson—himself a child of an alcoholic—remembers: "Even when we do try to get away from the hurt, we have a harder time succeeding at it because part of our minds remains locked into the woes at home."

Distracted by their family environments, children of alcoholics are less attentive in class. Their homework becomes less and less of a priority. Behavior changes. Teachers report that children of alcoholics are more likely to be hyperactive or delinquent. They also appear to have difficulty concentrating on school work and forming close relationships.

The child of one or both parents suffering from alcoholism may be well on the way to dropping out of school. The Children of Alcoholics Foundation reports that teenage children of alcoholics are three times more likely to be expelled from school or drop out due to early marriage, pregnancy, institutionalization, or military enlistment.

Forming relationships

For most children of alcoholics, embarrassment and shame about their home situations are barriers to forming relationships with peers. These young people often try to keep the alcoholism in their household a secret. Dolmetsch and Mauricette write:

> You get embarrassed when your parent comes home and passes out on the floor, or anywhere in the house for that matter, while a friend of yours is there. You get embarrassed when a friend is over at your house and your parent tries to pressure him or her into drinking.

Young people who fear that friends will learn about an alcoholic parent may have difficulty forming relationships. They worry about how others will view them. They worry, Dolmetsch and Mauricette write, "that other parents may not let their kids hang around you because it is too dangerous."

It is not uncommon for the spouse of an alcoholic to turn to the children for help in maintaining some kind of normalcy in the family. When these young people take on adult roles in the family, they feel different from their peers. The Children of Alcoholics Foundation reports:

> Some teenage children of alcoholics appear more resilient and are "mini-adults" who perform all functions well, but seem to experience little or no personal satisfaction in their successes.

These young people get used to living differ-

Many young people wrongly blame themselves for problems caused by a family member's alcoholism.

ently from their peers. They know how to do things that others their age have no experience with, like calling an ambulance when the alcoholic parent passes out or falls down the stairs. Likens encountered a young girl of two alcoholic parents who was indeed a mini-adult. The girl had a flow chart (a detailed, efficient work plan) tacked up on her bedroom wall, complete with schedules for taking out the garbage and doing the grocery shopping. "The nine-year-old was actually running the household," Likens says. Young people like this girl often have trouble relating to peers who do not have such daunting responsibilities.

In addition, many children of alcoholics fear that there is something wrong with them, and that no one would want to be their friend. They reason this is so because they come from such terrible homes, while others come from homes where life is more normal. Because children of alcoholics see themselves as being different from their peers, they tend to stay away from them. Dolmetsch and Mauricette explain this attitude from the viewpoint of a child of alcoholics:

> You don't give them a chance to get to know you. If you did, you are certain they would eventually see through you. They would see after a while that you are truly the rotten, stupid kid your parents already know you are anyway.

In addition to damaging the emotional stability of a family, there is evidence to suggest that alcohol contributes to physical violence in the home. There is no hard evidence that alcoholism actually causes physical abuse. Nonetheless, alcoholism is definitely a factor in many instances of domestic violence, especially against spouses. Numbers

A woman reveals through art the anger, terror, and physical pain of abuse she experienced as a child in an alcoholic family.

vary. Some studies indicate that alcoholism or alcohol abuse is involved in as many as 60 percent of spouse abuse cases. "Alcoholism accounts for between 25 percent and 50 percent of the violence committed between husbands and wives," writes author Herma Silverstein in *Alcoholism.*

Instances of violence between husband and wife leave their mark on children, who often witness these frightening scenes but are helpless to do anything about them.

Comedian Louie Anderson grew up in a family torn apart by an alcoholic parent. As quoted in his book *Dear Dad: Letters from an Adult Child*, a letter to Anderson's alcoholic father recalls the violence inflicted on his mother:

> I don't know what frightened us more. That you hit Mom, or that, once you sobered up and realized what had happened, you'd get drunk and angry all over again. Mom had a look on her face that seemed to say, "Oh, what am I going to do now?"

As much as spouses suffer from the violence of alcoholics, children suffer more. They are more defenseless. They do not have a lifetime of experience to help them cope with such situations. They are caught in a world of random violence where beatings come from those who are supposed to protect and nurture them. They quickly become distrustful of adults.

In *Teens Talk About Alcohol and Alcoholism*, Dolmetsch and Mauricette explain that the violence from alcoholic parents is for the most part caused by their lack of knowing what they are doing when they are drunk. "Some don't even know when they are abusing their kids. They are just bombed out of their minds and they do whatever their alcohol affected minds tell them to do."

An alcoholic parent's violence can explode at any moment—even when a child is trying to stay out of the way of it. Silverstein recalls the experi-

A young man recalls his childhood and the scene he witnessed often as the son of an alcoholic.

ence of Jean, a child of an alcoholic father. Jean's father stayed at home drinking all day, then beat Jean's mother, accusing her of seeing other men. "When Jean got in his way, he picked her up and threw her against a wall, twice causing her to be hospitalized."

Violence and drinking

Studies provide evidence of children suffering from violence at the hands of alcoholic parents. A 1983 report to Congress found that one out of three adult perpetrators of violence had been drinking before an abusive incident and that about 17 percent of all child abuse cases involved alcohol. In New York state alone, according to the New York State Council on Alcoholism, alcohol abuse is directly responsible for 70 percent of all child sexual abuse.

Alcoholism does not just lead to problems in the home. It is also a problem in the workplace. Employees suffering from alcoholism often arrive late to work or miss more days than other workers. Dr. Goodwin writes:

> Monday morning and Friday afternoon absenteeism, at least partly attributable to alcoholism, is so common that both industry and unions are considering a four-day work week (whereupon Tuesday morning or Thursday afternoon absenteeism will probably become common).

The work performance of alcoholics is also generally poor: they may make poor decisions, damage equipment, create friction with other workers, and may be involved in on-the-job accidents. According to the New York State Council on Alcoholism, in New York State alcoholism accounts for 40 percent of all fatal industrial accidents.

Further, when alcohol-related accidents occur, injured employees file worker's compensation claims, seeking financial help during recovery. These claims take a financial bite out of many companies. Fishman estimates that society pays a high cost for alcoholism in the workplace. He says the costs amount to about $120 billion each year:

> This figure includes not only the actual costs of treatment paid by insurance companies, but also the losses from work-related lateness, absenteeism, excessive health benefits, lowered productivity, and accidents, as well as those losses resulting from unemployment and disability insurance payouts.

Many businesses cope with alcoholic workers by dismissing them, but even then, business still suffers. The cost of looking for new workers, training them, and using other employees to fill in during that process can be high. The U.S. Department of Health and Human Services advises that the cost to replace a salaried worker is over $7,000; it can cost over $10,000 to replace a mid-level employee; and it can cost over $40,000 to replace a senior executive.

Community

Communities also feel the effects of alcoholism. In New York State, for example, the New York State Council on Alcoholism estimates that alcoholism accounts for 35 percent of all hospitalizations; 50 percent of all rapes, homicides, and fatal car crashes; 85 percent of deaths by fire; 68 percent of deaths by drowning; 25 percent of suicides; and 40 percent of family court actions.

Additionally, the cost of treating fetal alcohol syndrome can be an enormous economic burden

WHAT ALCOHOLISM COSTS SOCIETY
(In billions of dollars)

TOTAL

$116.6

Reduced Productivity — $65.7

Indirect Mortality — $18.1

Direct Treatment and Support — $14.8

Lost Employment — $5.3

Others — $12.7

Police and paramedics work quickly to rescue the victims of a traffic accident caused by a drunk driver. Alcohol-related traffic accidents claim about 18,000 lives a year.

on a community's medical services. According to the Children of Alcoholics Foundation, "The annual cost to the nation of treating 68,000 Fetal Alcohol Syndrome (FAS) children under the age of 18 is $670 million, and the cost of treating 160,000 FAS adults annually is $760 million."

Perhaps the greatest alcohol-related cost to a community, in both economic and human terms, comes from alcohol-related accidents and suicides. Traffic accidents, drownings, falls, and burns from fires are the leading causes of accidental death in the United States. Nearly half of all accidental deaths, suicides, and homicides are known to be alcohol related.

In 1988 the National Highway Traffic Safety Administration (NHTSA) defined a highway crash as being alcohol related when a driver has a blood alcohol level of 0.01 percent or above. While studies directly link alcohol drinking with impaired driving and traffic accidents, there has been little study of the links between alcoholism and traffic accidents.

Nonetheless, drunk driving takes a horrible toll. The American Council on Alcoholism reports that "alcohol-related traffic accidents claim about 18,000 lives each year."

Most drunk-driving accidents are caused by young drivers. The NHTSA reports that drivers sixteen to twenty-four years old represent only about 17 percent of all licensed drivers. They are involved in about 36 percent of all fatal alcohol-related crashes, however.

Alcohol consumption has been identified as even deadlier in other kinds of accidents. While there is as yet no strong evidence of a relationship between alcoholism and accidental deaths, researchers have established definite links between alcohol use and accidental drownings, falls, and burns.

FATAL ACCIDENTS INVOLVING DRUNK DRIVERS

Impaired drivers* per 100,000 licensed drivers

Age	16-24	25-44	45-64	65+
	16.7	10.3	3.7	1.6

*Blood alcohol level of .10% or more

Source: National Highway Transportation Safety Administration

A four-year study of the medical examiner's records in one New Jersey county indicated that a "history of alcohol problems or alcohol consumption immediately before a fatal accident occurred more often in deaths by falls and fires than in traffic deaths."

Suicide

Experts usually agree that suicides can be divided into two categories: impulsive and premeditated. Impulsive suicides happen on the spur of the moment, such as immediately after the breakup of a relationship or the death of a parent or sibling. A premeditated suicide has been thought out and planned.

Recent research indicates that suicide and alcohol use are linked more often in impulsive suicides. Why this is so is not clear. A 1990 report to Congress notes:

> Research indicates that 20 to 30 percent of suicide victims have a history of alcohol abuse or were drinking shortly before their suicides, and that alcohol tends to be associated with suicides that are impulsive rather than premeditated.

Researchers have found what appears to be another kind of link between alcoholism and suicide. Although this research is still in the early stages, researchers have observed that some teenagers who commit suicide also have at least one parent who is an alcoholic. According to the Children of Alcoholics Foundation, "Preliminary reports show a relationship between parental alcoholism and adolescent suicide. . . ." The nature of this relationship is unclear, however. Research continues in an effort to learn more.

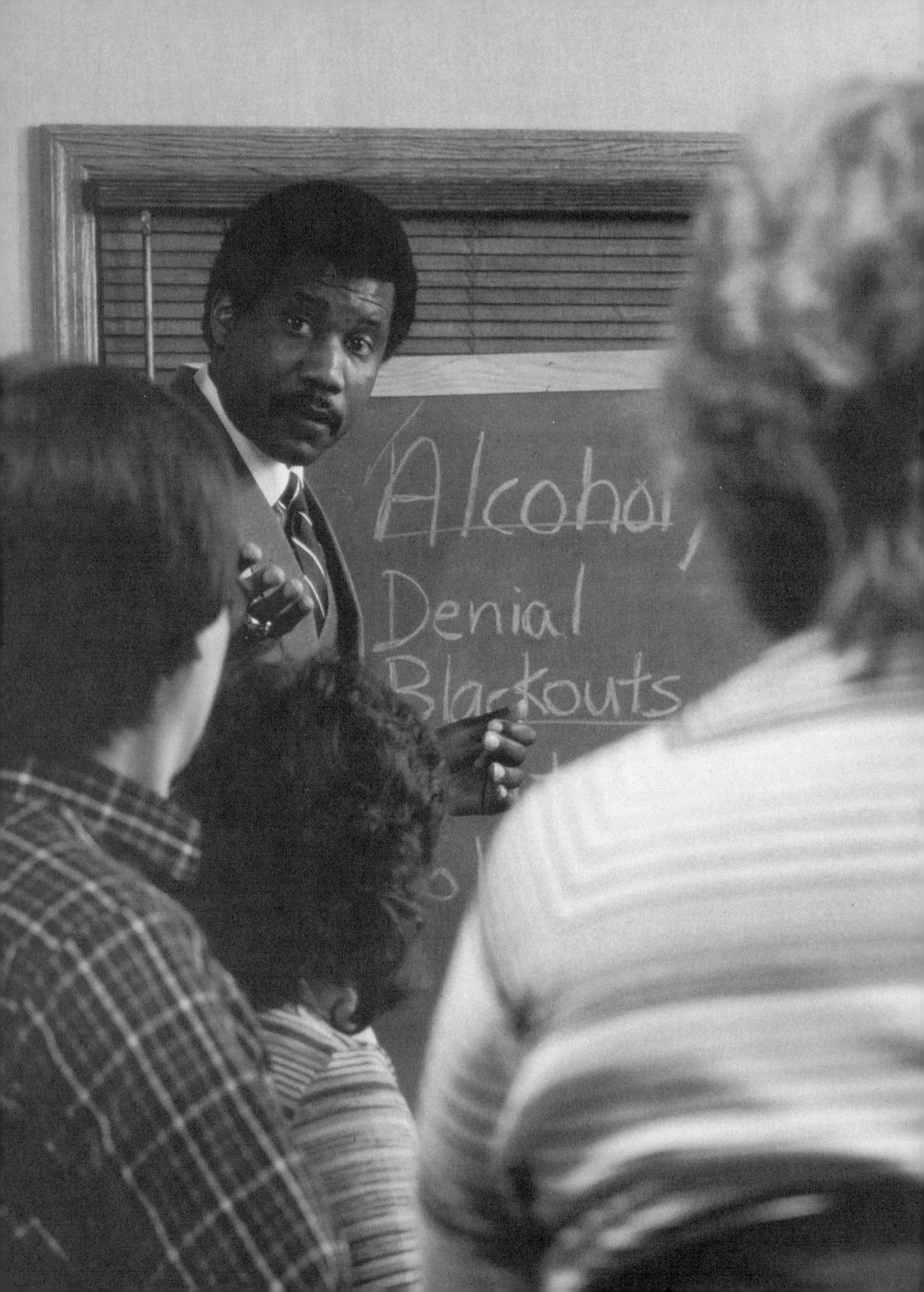
Alcohol
Denial
Blackouts

5

Treatment

SOMETIMES THE MOST difficult aspect of alcoholism treatment is for alcoholics to admit they have a problem. Some alcoholics simply think of themselves as social drinkers. They do not realize that they have developed a dependence on alcohol and so they deny that they even have a problem.

Friends and family who urge an alcoholic to seek treatment usually meet with resistance. Alcoholics do not want to discuss their problem—it is too painful. By refusing to listen to anything having to do with alcoholism, alcoholics are able to deny that alcohol controls much of their lives and that they have lost the ability to drink in moderation.

Even when alcoholics admit they might have a problem, many will insist that they can treat themselves. According to the American Council on Alcoholism:

> It is a tremendous task to repair the damage done in all these areas yourself. . . . Alcoholism is an illness that responds to enlightened treatment by doctors, therapists, clergy and Alcoholics Anonymous. It is possible, although extremely difficult, to stop drinking without outside help. But why do it alone when help is available? It might be more profitable to use your energy and determination to work along with the people who can help you.

(Opposite page) Recovering alcoholics attend a treatment group. Treatment for alcoholics often includes classes and emotional support from other recovering alcoholics.

Most experts agree that alcoholism cannot really be cured. That is, alcoholism is not a disease like early stage cancer, which may be attacked and destroyed by surgery, chemotherapy, and radiation. There is no antibiotic for alcoholism; nor is there a wonder drug to wash it away.

In most cases alcoholism cannot be cured, because of its chronic, or continuing, nature. The symptoms may go away as treatment progresses, but the individual has only controlled the alcoholism, not eliminated it. As the New York State Clearinghouse on Alcohol Information explains, "The disease is in remission as long as the alcoholic person doesn't use alcohol."

For this reason most alcoholics cannot go back to being social drinkers. Alcoholism, most experts agree, cannot be cured by simply altering drinking habits. As the National Institute for Alcohol Abuse and Alcoholism states:

> Most counselors and recovered alcoholic persons believe that if the alcoholic individual who has given up drinking thinks he will be able to handle alcohol again, he may slip back repeatedly into drunkenness.

Alcoholism can be treated

While it cannot be cured, alcoholism can be treated. Most methods of treatment try to give recovering alcoholics skills for coping with problems so that they do not turn to alcohol. Alcoholics benefit from treatment much in the same way that sufferers of other incurable diseases benefit from treatment. For example, there is no cure for diabetes. Yet there are excellent treatments available that allow diabetics to live productive, satisfying lives.

Alcoholism may be treated in several ways, including hospitalization, therapy, and self-help groups. Many alcoholics eventually turn to these various treatment programs. The National Institute for Alcohol Abuse and Alcoholism reports that, in a twelve-month period ending in October 1987, almost 1.5 million clients were treated in 5,586 alcoholism treatment units around the country. And statistics show that treatment for alcoholism works: between one-third and two-thirds of all people who seek help recover from alcoholism.

Success, though, can be achieved only if the alcoholic wants it; those who don't want to be treated usually remain active alcoholics. In this respect alcoholism is like any other disease for which treatment is available. If a sick person does not take medication regularly or refuses to exercise or stick to a prescribed diet, the treatment will not work. It is the same with alcoholism.

In order to begin treatment, alcoholics must get

A support group for teenagers from alcoholic families gives these young people an opportunity to express their feelings and develop coping skills.

Two residents of a Michigan halfway house attend a meeting for alcoholics. Halfway houses allow recovering alcoholics to live in a household setting and have the mutual support they need to refrain from drinking.

beyond their resistance to treatment; this resistance can be challenged by various methods, including family intervention and employee and student assistance programs.

Confronting the problem

In an effort to get alcoholics to acknowledge their problem and thus take the first step toward accepting treatment, family members can confront the alcoholic with the drinking problem. The family members usually recount specific details of harmful alcohol-influenced behavior and how this behavior affected—and continues to affect—them. This process is called family intervention. Alcoholism programs and agencies can provide guidance for families during this process.

Workplace programs called employee assistance programs, or EAPs, also confront alcoholics with their problem and urge them to seek help. Today, almost every large corporation in America has an EAP.

Employee assistance programs use a variety of techniques. Most rely on specially trained staff or peer counselors. Staff and counselors often refer employees with alcohol problems to organizations and agencies that deal extensively with alcoholism treatment and counseling.

There is little hard evidence to verify the number of alcoholic workers who have turned their lives around because of EAPs. But experts believe that EAPs work. Ross Fishman states that "these programs have been quite successful."

Assisting students

School-based programs, called student assistance programs, or SAPs, reach students at their schools. A trained SAP counselor usually sees students who are referred by teachers, school

Former first lady Nancy Reagan appears moved by the tales of suffering shared at a meeting of General Motors employees who are recovering alcoholics. Alcoholism has cost industry millions of dollars in lost productivity.

nurses, or guidance counselors. Besides school staff, friends often refer the student. Too often, students in trouble with alcohol will keep denying they have a problem; it often takes another person to push them into taking action. SAPs also can help students who have problems with alcoholic family members.

Bottoming out

The various methods of intervention try to catch the alcoholic early. But for many alcoholics the first acknowledgment that something is really wrong comes only with a terrible event such as losing a job, losing a family, or having a serious car accident.

Sometimes it can take a death for an alcoholic to realize that something is really wrong. In their book *Teens Talk About Alcohol and Alcoholism*, Paul Dolmetsch and Gail Mauricette summarize the story of Joe, an alcoholic:

> Joe is a stepfather. One night he comes home drunk and goes into his stepsons' room. He wakes up the older one and begins to hit him. His stepson hits his head on the bedframe and goes into convulsions. His mother wakes up from all the racket. She rushes her son to the hospital, where he dies from internal bleeding. Joe is arrested and charged. He is so distraught from what he has done that he seeks help, finally, on his own.

This is often the kind of event that gets an alcoholic into treatment. The alcoholic has, in a sense, "bottomed out." The damage wrought by drinking has finally become clear.

Detoxification

Someone who has reached bottom often needs immediate help, and this usually means detoxification, or "detox." Detox is the necessary first step in treatment of alcoholism. Alcoholics go through detox to rid their bodies of alcohol.

Under normal, nonalcoholism conditions detoxification is performed by a person's liver in a day or so. But alcoholics usually have a large amount of alcohol in their bloodstreams—larger than the liver can manage to detoxify at a normal rate. In cases of severe alcoholism it usually takes about five days before alcohol is out of the patient's system.

Detoxification is an uncomfortable experience. The body's cells have gotten used to functioning with alcohol, and they respond as the alcohol is diminished during the detox process. Fishman describes what happens during detox: "Such symptoms as sweating, nervous tremors, rapid heart rate, and increased blood pressure appear. A hangover, which is really a kind of 'mini-withdrawal,' is far less severe." The patient undergoing detox usually experiences hallucinations, delirium, and disturbed sleep.

Alcoholics who have serious medical and psychological symptoms often undergo detox at a hospital detoxification unit. There, they receive a complete physical checkup to identify physical problems that will have to be monitored while detox occurs. During the period of detox they receive drugs intended to counter the effects of withdrawal and of the damage by alcohol on their bodies. They are often given Librium and Valium, two drugs that help manage withdrawal effects. They also receive high-strength vitamins for the gastric problems that commonly occur during detox. Because some alcoholics experience anxiety, depression, and confusion during this time, specialized counseling is also usually available.

For most alcoholics, though, detox does not require hospitalization. Outpatient detox, which may be completed in five to twelve days, is usually suitable for alcoholics who are not severely dependent on alcohol and are in otherwise good

An alcoholic undergoing treatment at a hospital faces a harsh reality as his body detoxifies from alcohol.

Treatment groups like this one help alcoholics learn new ways of coping with the stresses of life so that they will not seek to escape their problems through alcohol.

health. Their withdrawal symptoms are much less severe then those of patients at the more advanced stages of alcoholism.

After detox has been completed and medical problems are under control, alcoholics look to longer-term efforts to change their destructive behavior patterns. Today there are many different approaches designed to keep the alcoholic off alcohol and help the alcoholic solve problems without alcohol. Some of these treatments include drug treatment, therapy, and self-help groups.

Antabuse

Antabuse is the product name of the drug disulfiram and is the most widely used drug treatment for recovering alcoholics. Antabuse is often prescribed for patients who have just undergone detox and treatment of their alcohol-related medical problems.

For Antabuse treatment the patient visits a physician—often every day—to receive the medication, which is taken several times during the day. The patient knows that if the Antabuse is combined with alcohol, violent headaches and nausea will occur. Author Herma Silverstein contends that Antabuse is a powerful incentive for a person not to drink. She quotes a recovering alcoholic as saying, "I still wanted a drink . . . but with that stuff in me, I knew I didn't have to decide fifty times a day anymore."

Of course the patient may choose not to ingest the Antabuse on any given day. But many believe that having to choose is one of the great benefits of Antabuse treatment: because the patient sees the physician on a regular basis and has to decide to take the drug every day, willpower to resist drinking is developed. Many authorities believe that this willpower is necessary to stop drinking altogether.

Psychological therapy

Therapy helps alter long-term behavior so that the alcoholic finds better patterns of behavior than resorting to alcohol. Several types of therapy are available to recovering alcoholics, and they are conducted individually or in groups, and usually by professionals.

In therapy patients learn to admit they have problems and to feel strong enough about themselves to tackle life without alcohol. An important part of individual therapy is developing trust in another person—the therapist. As the National Institute on Alcohol Abuse and Alcoholism explains, the alcoholic is often "lonely, full of guilt, and burdened by many disappointments." For the alcoholic the therapist, in a sense, replaces alcohol as a rock of dependability for getting through difficult times.

Not all alcoholics, though, are able to enter into this one-on-one relationship with a therapist; for them, group therapy or family therapy may be more appropriate. In group therapy several alcoholics join together under the guidance of a therapist. The alcoholics build trust through their interactions with each other and their therapist.

In family therapy families come together under the supervision of a therapist to discuss family problems. Often family members learn to admit that they are not completely responsible for all the problems in their lives. Author Janet Grosshandler quotes a young man named George, who went with his mother and father twice a week to see a therapist:

> We all needed to straighten things out in our heads and get along better. The groups helped us face our problems, and I was able to see that I wasn't the absolute cause of our family breakdown, maybe more the result of it.

Finally, self-help groups meet and provide support among members and their families without the presence of professional alcoholism coun-

A drug counselor meets with a young alcoholic for a one-to-one therapy session. Meeting alone with a counselor for therapy is one of many methods used during treatment for alcoholism.

An Alcoholics Anonymous group meets. AA's now-famous Twelve Steps and Twelve Traditions are posted on the wall behind the speaker.

selors. These groups stress the importance of peer counseling—friendship, devotion, and understanding among those suffering from alcoholism. Members—who are alcoholics and recovering alcoholics—make themselves available at any time of day or night for fellow members struck by the sudden urge to have a drink.

Alcoholics Anonymous

The best-known self-help alcoholism treatment program is Alcoholics Anonymous (AA). It is a supportive group that can complement the efforts of individual and family therapy and counseling.

Alcoholics Anonymous has proven to be enormously popular. It was started in 1932 in Akron, Ohio, by two men, Bill Wilson and Dr. Robert Holbrook Smith. Four years later AA had only about one hundred members. Today AA has about two million members in thousands of groups in 136 countries. Two offshoots of Alcoholics Anonymous have also met with success: Alateen, for teenage children of alcoholics, and Al-Anon, which provides help for families and friends of alcoholics. All three organizations are free, confidential, and open to anyone with an alcohol-related problem.

An important phrase that members of Alcoholics Anonymous learn to use is "one day at a time." For most people trying to achieve anything difficult all at once is overwhelming and doomed to fail. When they feel the urge to drink, members tell themselves they must fight it for a minute; when that minute is up, they battle for another minute, and so on. Members of AA fight small battles against their own urge to drink with an eye toward winning the war against their alcoholism.

Support from others

Members of AA find that they gain enormous confidence from the presence and support of other members. Recalls one recovering alcoholic, "If all the people in this room with me have stayed sober; if they have found the ways to do it; then I must be able to do it, too!"

Meetings are held in churches and synagogues, corporation boardrooms and public schools, on ships and in prisons. During these meetings recovering drinkers speak about the difficulties they have had with alcoholism and their attempts to stop drinking. Others listen attentively and are enthusiastic in their support and advice.

One important feature of Alcoholics Anonymous is its spiritual approach to solving alcoholism. Members of AA call their organization a fellowship, which means "a group of men and women called together by God." The person joining AA admits that he or she has no power over the addiction; also, individuals place faith in a being greater than themselves to help fight the temptation to drink.

Other self-help groups

Some alcoholics have trouble, though, with the spiritual aspects of Alcoholics Anonymous and turn to other self-help groups, like Rational Recovery Systems, or RR.

Rational Recovery has a basically simple view of how alcoholics can keep from drinking. Rather than relying on a higher power for support and strength, RR contends that because drinking is a purposeful activity (drinkers *decide* to take a drink), an individual can make the decision *not* to drink and stick by it. Using the principles of a type of therapy called rational-emotive therapy, alcoholics learn to recognize and combat their own "addictive voice." By abiding by the decision not to drink, they can consider themselves recovered from alcoholism. They do not need to attend self-help meetings for support and encouragement after they have stopped drinking.

Established in California in 1987, RR is, in the words of its founder Jack Trimpey (himself a "recovered" alcoholic), for "people who are not interested in spiritual life. We're a group of people who won't be told what to think or what to believe—and we have better things to do with sobriety than waste it on recovery." This concept has been gaining in popularity. RR groups are held in about 350 cities around the United States.

There is as yet no proof for determining which alcoholism treatment program is best. While treatment programs in general have been shown to be effective, no studies have proven that there are significantly higher success rates in any one kind of treatment over other kinds. Also, there is no proof as yet to indicate how much time must

Jack Trimpey founded the Rational Recovery (RR) treatment program in 1987. He believes alcoholics have the power within themselves to stop drinking.

be spent in a treatment program for the program to be effective. It appears that the efficiency of any particular program depends at least as much on the patient's efforts as on the program.

Patient-treatment matching

Researchers have found that those with alcohol problems often respond better to a treatment program matched to their specific needs. This is usually referred to as patient-treatment matching. For instance, veterans with drinking problems often do well at Veterans Administration hospitals where counselors, staff members, and other personnel are usually all veterans of military service. They have a sympathetic bond of shared experience between them and the patients they serve.

Treatment can also be tailored to a specific group. Faced with rising rates of alcoholism among their people, native American groups dealing with alcoholism have come up with a new approach that is really a very old approach: the sweat lodge. The sweat lodge is the most common purification ceremony used by native North Americans.

Once a month in Tecumseh, Oklahoma, Kenneth Coosewoon, director of the Apache Drop-In Center, enters a tarp-covered tent with about eighteen young alcoholism patients of the nearby Central Oklahoma Juvenile Detention Center. The tent is filled with steam from steaming rocks at the center, and Coosewoon and the youngsters "sing songs in the dark to the Great Spirit, drumming, praying and receiving counseling for the problems they dare to talk about."

The defenses of the young patients are broken down by their togetherness, communion in their native language, and the heat, which shoots up over one hundred degrees. This treatment has helped adolescents from different backgrounds

The sweat lodge is a traditional native American method of purification, bonding, and spirituality. It has proven effective as a treatment for alcoholism among some native Americans.

but has been most effective with native American youths. Camille Palmer, the detention center's drug and alcohol treatment coordinator, says: "With the sweat we seem to reach the native American kids in a way our traditional methods of psychology can't, even among kids who have been totally removed from their culture."

It may be that the spirituality of the sweat lodge is the major factor in its success. If so, this seems to recall the spiritual aspect of Alcoholics Anonymous. Whatever the reason, specially designed treatment programs like the sweat lodge are finding more popularity in the treatment of alcoholism.

Recovery begins the moment an alcoholic stops drinking. According to the National Council on Alcoholism and Drug Dependence, more than 1.5 million Americans are currently in recovery from alcoholism. The time it takes for alcoholics and their families to recover from the wounds of alcoholism is different for each family.

Avoiding relapse

During the initial recovery period the family and alcoholic are still under pressure. The alcoholic has maddening urges to sneak a drink—and sometimes does. Family members often think that life will be perfect when the alcoholic stops drinking—and it never is. They may push too hard for the alcoholic to get better, and tension and anxiety are ever present. The alcoholic may want a drink again. In the book *Teens Talk About*

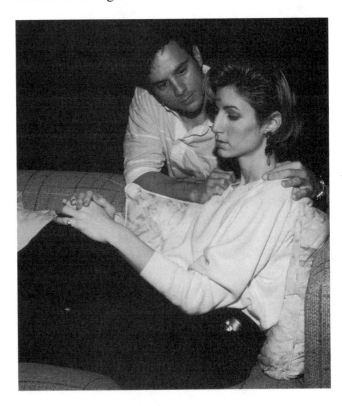

Family members console each other during a crisis. The road to recovery is long and often difficult. Troubles caused by alcoholism do not immediately end when an alcoholic stops drinking.

Alcohol and Alcoholism, one recovering alcoholic admits that "a lot of it depends on my mood. If I am under stress and strain, I might want a drink more than at other times."

Even those who have successfully stayed away from alcohol for a number of years may suddenly begin to drink again (go into relapse). The psychological effect of relapse can be devastating. A relapse can cause alcoholics to lose their dignity and self-esteem and feel so bad that they never stop drinking again. Alcoholics Anonymous stresses that those who relapse should understand that it is not the end of the world—the relapse is only part of their illness.

As Dr. Stanley E. Gitlow, associate clinical professor of medicine at Mt. Sinai Medical School in New York, explains:

> Obviously, [the alcoholic] has to be given something to replace the "oral magic," and the only thing I know is a helping hand. The helping hand may be Alcoholics Anonymous or psychotherapy; it may be the clergyman, the social worker, or the physician. The alcoholic needs people who understand and are compassionate, who offer the ear, the time, and the hand to help him through all his discomfort.

6

Prevention

BECAUSE ALCOHOLISM IS caused by a combination of physical and environmental factors, its prevention also requires a combined approach. One way to prevent alcoholism is to keep alcohol out of people's hands. In other times and places this strategy has proven to be effective. In the 1930s, while Prohibition caused a lot of people to drink on the sly in private clubs, it also kept many Americans away from alcohol, and the incidence of alcoholism was greatly reduced. In some regions of the world, including parts of the Middle East, the sale and consumption of alcohol is banned and alcoholism is relatively unknown. In America today, some authorities say raising taxes on alcohol will make it simply too costly for many drinkers, and this measure, like Prohibition, will keep alcohol from the public and thus lower the alcoholism rate.

Most experts agree, though, that in societies that accept the use of alcohol, education is the key to the prevention of alcohol abuse. Most people who learn that they are doing bad things to themselves and others can be counted on to stop doing those things. Experts feel that education at an early age regarding alcoholism and drinking is the best way to prevent future problems. Early education is, as the American Coun-

(Opposite page) A student group meets after school to discuss drinking and driving and other issues related to alcohol abuse.

cil on Alcoholism states, "currently the best known method to create a knowledge base upon which a young person can make responsible decisions about drinking in the future."

Education efforts come from various sources, including schools, the media, business, government, and the home.

Schools

Studies indicate that teenagers will try alcohol despite programs that urge them not to. A 1989 study by researcher J. M. Moskowitz supports this view. This study found that "there has been little consistent evidence suggesting that specific approaches change attitudes or delay or prevent alcohol use."

However, studies also show that school-based

A teacher and student discuss a school campaign to promote awareness about alcohol and drug abuse. Posters hung around campus remind students of the dangers of alcohol abuse.

alcohol education programs seem to be successful in educating students about alcohol. Experts interpret this as a good sign. This means that students equipped with information will be more capable of making sound drinking decisions. A 1990 report to Congress concluded that "most approaches seem to have a positive effect on knowledge." Today students begin getting information in school about alcohol and other drugs as early as the first grade.

The most common place for students to receive alcohol prevention information is in driver education classes. Goals of these and other classes are to educate students about drinking and driving, as well as to try to change students' attitudes towards alcohol and teach them values and decision-making skills that will help them decide against abusing alcohol.

An important strategy for alcohol abuse prevention is the training of student peer teachers, who organize discussion groups and conduct classes on drug and alcohol abuse. Research has supported the view that peer pressure is central to students' decisions about drinking. In 1972, researcher R. Jessor reported that peer pressure was the most important factor "accounting for the initiation of drinking by previously abstaining high school students." Many alcohol prevention programs are organized into student-led, high school-based chapters to provide peer support not to drink.

Students reach out

Students Against Driving Drunk (SADD) is a nationwide organization with thousands of chapters in public schools across the country. It was started by a teacher who had lost two of his students in drunk-driving accidents. SADD's motto, "Friends don't let friends drive drunk," became a national slogan.

(Right) Student members of Students Against Driving Drunk attend a meeting to discuss what they can do to prevent alcohol-related traffic accidents.
(Below) Candy Lightner, founder of Mothers Against Drunk Driving, poses in her Sacramento, California, office with a picture of her daughter. Lightner's daughter was thirteen when she was killed by a drunk driver.

Besides training students to offset peer pressure to drink, one of the main features of SADD is a contract that parents and teenagers sign. Called the Contract for Life, it appears as a legal contract with spaces for the signatures of the parent and the teen. The teenager agrees to call on the parent any time when faced with the possibility of a drunk-driving situation. The parent agrees, in writing, to come to the child's aid—and also to avoid getting into the same situation.

Mothers act

Another organization working on alcoholism prevention is Mothers Against Drunk Driving, or MADD. MADD was founded in 1980 by Candy Lightner. Lightner's thirteen-year-old daughter was killed by a drunk driver in California. The organization has many chapters around the country and has successfully urged passage of tough laws and stiff penalties for drunk drivers.

MADD believes that education is crucial to preventing alcoholism. In 1992 MADD's national president, Mickey Sadoff, declared that MADD teaches students that "not only is it illegal to drink if you're under 21, it's also unsafe for anyone to drive under the influence of alcohol or other drugs."

MADD also tries to spread its influence into the nation's schools by cosponsoring, with the Aetna Life and Casualty Insurance Company, an annual nationwide poster-essay contest for students in grades one through twelve. The theme of the 1992 contest was "Make All The Right Moves—Drive Sober." The contest is one way students get to exercise their creativity while making peers and parents aware of the dangers of using alcohol and other drugs while driving.

Through a resource network named TARGET,

Relatives of those killed by drunk drivers look for photos of their loved ones displayed at a 1990 Washington, D.C., news conference held to mark the tenth anniversary of MADD.

teachers, school administrators, and student leaders and athletes play an important part in trying to teach students about the negative effects of drug and alcohol abuse. TARGET is a service component of the National Federation of State High School Associations.

While teachers with TARGET training have specific strategies for communicating information on alcohol, they are also taught to stress the importance of a healthy life-style as an alternative to alcohol and drug abuse. For example, in 1992, TARGET assisted the National Hockey League in teaching inner-city youth about ice hockey and life. Players first taught the youths that a player in the defending zone is not allowed to shoot the puck the entire length of the ice—this is known as "icing." In hockey care must be taken to keep the puck under control and move it properly along the ice, and not just fling it aimlessly away. Then the players followed with this message:

A hockey player teaches inner-city youths the fundamentals of hockey while also teaching them about the ills of drug abuse. The programs is sponsored by the National Hockey League and the National Federation of State High School Associations.

In life, keeping ourselves under control is very important if we want to achieve success. We may not always be able to control the outcome of a life situation, but we can always stay in control of ourselves.

Two billboard advertisements along a New York highway seem to demonstrate the contradictory messages given to young people about drinking.

Media

According to the media watchdog Alcohol Research Information Service, $1.2 billion was spent by the alcohol industry in media advertising in 1989. Some people maintain that these media messages challenge the best alcohol prevention efforts. These messages, usually in the form of advertisements on television, in the movies, on radio and on billboards, often encourage the consumption of alcohol. Author Janet Grosshandler summarizes the attitudes of these messages: "It's fun! It makes you popular! You'll feel great and forget your troubles! You will have romance and love if you drink with your date, boyfriend, girlfriend! Drinking will make you cool! Promises, promises, promises. . . ."

At the same time they often breeze over or totally ignore the problems associated with alco-

The cast from "Cheers," a popular television series. All episodes of the series take place in a fictitious bar.

holism. Business and industry, though limited by federal laws, advertise alcoholic beverages as, basically, a "legal good time." Sex appeal, too, is used to sell alcoholic beverages on billboards and in magazines.

On television, the most popular entertainment medium, intoxicated characters are still regularly portrayed as jolly, essentially harmless persons. Popular shows feature scenes taking place in bars where nearly every topic but one—alcoholism— is open to comment and discussion. Critics say that this gives the message to viewers that drinking and its associated behavior are acceptable and even expected in many social situations. Author Herbert Fingarette notes one study that revealed that on television "the beverage most often consumed is distilled liquor, while in real life only about 16 percent of the beverages drunk by Americans are alcoholic."

There is really no hard proof stating that media

messages cause or affect alcoholism. According to the American Council on Alcoholism, "there is no reliable basis on which to conclude that alcohol advertising significantly affects alcohol abuse or the overall consumption of alcohol beverages."

Nevertheless, some groups and individuals have called for the media to be more aware of and even change its messages about alcohol and drinking. About three quarters of adults favor health warnings on alcoholic beverage advertisements, according to an *Advertising Age*-Gallup poll. The same poll found that almost half felt alcohol advertising should be banned.

Sometimes requests for change become more desperate—and more than mere requests. In 1991 in Harlem, New York City, the Reverend Calvin Butts, a local minister, began defacing and tearing down billboards in the community that promoted beer. The minister, backed by members of his congregation and community, declared to the media that the alcoholic-beverage companies involved in the advertising were targeting young blacks because they were supposedly more susceptible to drinking and would provide additional revenue to the alcohol industry.

The company responsible for the billboards argued that they had the right to advertise wherever they wanted to and that targeting young blacks was a marketing strategy, not a show of prejudice. In the end, though, the company agreed to curtail its advertising in the community.

Business and government

Business and government are also responding to the problem of alcoholism. Many businesses, especially bars, taverns, and restaurants, are making use of server-training programs offered by outside agencies. Also, the alcohol industry has gotten involved in abuse prevention.

A bartender pours another round of drinks for a customer. Many bartenders and servers are now trained to intervene when a customer has had too much to drink.

In server training, alcohol servers—bartenders and waiters—are being taught how to intervene with customers who may become a threat to themselves and others by their drinking. The hope is that server training will help cut down on some alcohol-related problems, such as fights and driving accidents, occurring both inside and outside of drinking establishments. By modifying or changing the behavior of their servers, businesses hope to affect the way people drink.

Businesses have had a real financial interest in setting up server-training programs: According to the 1990 *Special Report to the U. S. Congress on Alcohol and Health*, "thirty-five states have . . . laws that allow an individual injured by a drinker who was served alcohol illegally while intoxicated to sue the server of the alcohol for recovery of damages."

Studies show that server training has had a

Most of the large alcoholic beverage companies, particularly brewers of popular beers, actively campaign for responsible use of their products. The Miller Brewing Company provided this reminder at an outdoor public event it sponsored.

positive effect on those individuals with whom servers come into direct contact. A 1987 study by R. F. Saltz found that per capita alcohol consumption was not affected but that

> the probability of a customer's becoming intoxicated was cut in half . . . after servers had been trained to monitor for potential intoxication based on amount of alcohol consumed, rate of consumption, and customer weight.

Also, a 1987 study by researcher E. S. Geller showed that, because servers can tailor their actions to each individual drinker, they are thought to be more influential on the whole than some other kinds of prevention efforts.

TEAM

Server training is also being used in sports arenas. One community-based server training program was instituted in 1987 by several corporations, including CBS Television, GEICO Insurance, and the National Basketball Association. This program, called the Techniques of Effective Alcohol Management (TEAM) project, worked in seven arenas around the United States to keep the arena environment enjoyable for all spectators by finding and containing those exhibiting drunken behavior and also by watching for drunk driving after the event. In these arenas workers in beverage and food services, security, ushering, and other positions were trained to spot and intervene with individuals showing alcohol impairment. Impaired individuals would be given a ride home. The program is a recent one, and while there are no statistics proving its effectiveness, many have applauded its efforts.

Businesses that produce alcoholic beverages have attempted to join the prevention efforts. One such company is Anheuser-Busch, which makes Budweiser beer and other alcoholic beverages.

Due to the nature of their business, alcoholic-beverage companies lean heavily toward promoting the idea of stopping alcohol abuse—as opposed to the idea of abstaining from alcohol altogether.

Anheuser-Busch has initiated several kinds of programs, some designed to prevent alcohol abuse and others for those with alcohol-related problems. A recent full-page Anheuser-Busch advertisement in the *San Diego Union-Tribune* and other newspapers drew attention to these programs. For example, Alert Cab is a program offering free rides home from taverns and bars for those too drunk to drive. Also, T.I.P.S. (Training for Intervention Procedures by Servers of Alcohol) is Anheuser-Busch's version of a server-training program.

Warning labels

By making it mandatory that warning labels be put on all alcoholic beverages to warn users of the harmful effects of alcohol, government is also playing a role in alcoholism prevention efforts.

All bottles and containers holding alcoholic beverages and labeled after November 1989 must have health and safety warning labels. Some of these labels warn that alcohol should not be consumed by pregnant women because of the possibility of birth defects. Other labels warn that alcohol consumption impairs judgment and driving ability and may cause health problems.

Punitive measures are used by government, too. These measures are concrete reminders of unacceptable and dangerous alcohol-related behavior. One punitive preventative measure used by government assigns stiff penalties to drunk drivers.

Today drunk drivers are likely to be ordered to perform community service, pay a substantial fine, serve time in jail, or a combination of these. This stiff sentencing is meant to warn potential

Federal law now requires all alcoholic beverage containers to include warnings to consumers of the dangers of drinking alcohol.

drunk drivers of the possible consequences of their actions, and this warning seems to have been heeded. A 1988 study by researcher P. L. Zador concludes that laws revoking or suspending licenses of drunk drivers, as well as laws for mandatory jail terms or community service for first offenders, were among factors that "played a role in the decline of fatal alcohol-related crashes in the early 1980s."

Drunk drivers are not the only ones penalized for their actions. Within the past few years court decisions in some states have held hosts who served visibly drunk guests additional alcohol to be responsible for alcohol-related damages—especially auto accidents that occurred later. These rulings communicate to hosts and others who serve alcohol at parties that they, too, are responsible for the drinker who gets behind the wheel.

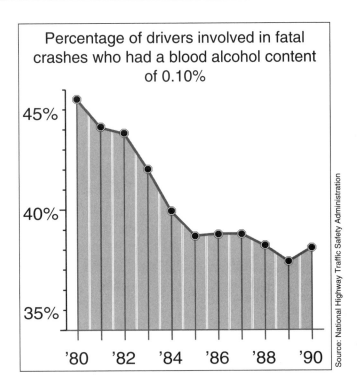

Percentage of drivers involved in fatal crashes who had a blood alcohol content of 0.10%

Source: National Highway Traffic Safety Administration

The home is probably the most important educational environment. This is the place where children begin learning—well before they are ready for school. Parents may be the primary source for information and teaching attitudes about alcohol and alcoholism. Many experts believe that parental example and discipline work best for most young people.

In some families, family rituals may promote better emotional adjustment and prevent alcohol abuse. Family rituals are things a family does together in a certain way or on a regular basis, such as eating dinner together or going out for a Sunday picnic.

Family rituals seem to teach children to see things through and to make sacrifices to achieve something worthy. According to a March 11, 1992, article in the *New York Times,* part of the power of family rituals "appears to be in offering children a sense of stability and security, dependable anchors despite chaos in other areas of family life."

Two studies done by Dr. Linda Bennett, an anthropologist, were carried out on children having at least one alcoholic parent. The studies confirmed that among these children, those involved in family rituals—such as eating dinner every night with their parents and siblings—were much less likely to become adult alcoholics or marry an alcoholic spouse.

"If you grow up in a family with strong rituals, you're more likely to be resilient as an adult," says Dr. Steven J. Wolin, a psychiatrist at the Family Research Center at George Washington University.

Sometimes an alcoholism-prevention program can be used to teach family members specific strategies to help prevent alcohol abuse. One program gaining popularity with parents is Talking

Family rituals like regularly eating dinner together provide stability and security for children. Some studies show that children from families who have such rituals are less likely to abuse alcohol as adults.

With Your Kids About Alcohol, or TWYKAA. TWYKAA is run by the Prevention Research Institute, a nonprofit corporation in Lexington, Kentucky, and was recognized as one of the U.S. Office of Substance Abuse Prevention's Twenty Exemplary Programs in 1987.

The TWYKAA program goal is prevention for a lifetime, not just during teen years. It focuses on increasing abstinence, delaying any use of alcohol, and reducing high-risk use of alcohol. In a four-session program parents are given new information to share with their children about alcohol, including how to estimate biological risk for alcoholism. They are also taught skills needed to discuss alcohol with their children.

Evaluations indicate that the TWYKAA program has been successful. Research showed that the program increased abstinence and decreased

A parent reads to her children, helping them to build strong minds and a strong emotional base from which decisions can be made.

high-risk drinking for both parents and their children. An early evaluation found that alcohol use decreased among some of the adolescents whose parents took the TWYKAA course.

What it all comes down to is the goal of a family working as a supportive and involved unit to help build strong minds and a strong emotional base from which decisions can be made. This means that families have to work together and that throughout their work at least two important lessons should be imparted: that drinking should never be an expected or required behavior and that armed with the helpful and accurate information from a concerned society and the love and support of a determined family, young people can learn enough about alcoholism to prevent it.

Glossary

Alcoholics Anonymous: A worldwide organization of recovering alcoholics. Members meet to talk about their alcohol-related problems and encourage one another to stay abstinent.

Antabuse: The most widely used drug treatment. Antabuse is the trade name of the drug disulfiram and is swallowed several times per day, according to medical prescription. If alcohol is then consumed, the patient suffers from violent headaches and extreme nausea.

blackout: Being unable to remember what one said or did while under the influence of alcohol.

cirrhosis: Fibrous, fatty scar tissue developing on the liver after a long period of drinking. Cirrhosis can block blood flow through the liver and cause death.

delirium tremens (DTs): Trembling, nausea, hallucinations, and insomnia caused by sudden withdrawal of alcohol from an addicted body. Severe DTs can lead to death.

detoxification: The process of eliminating a toxic substance, like alcohol, from the body.

drug: Anything a person can take into his or her system that has an effect on how the mind or body works.

fetal alcohol syndrome (FAS): A term used to describe the damage some unborn children suffer from the alcohol consumed by their mothers during pregnancy. This damage is in the form of growth deficiency, mental retardation, facial abnormalities, and other birth defects.

genetic predisposition: A genetic tendency toward alcoholism as a result of a history of alcoholism in the drinker's family.

hangover: The ill feeling most people have several hours after having been drunk. Headaches are common to the hangover and are caused by the swelling, from alcohol, of blood vessels in the brain.

peer pressure: The strong influence of members of a social circle on any one of its members.

Prohibition: Period in America between 1919 and 1933 when the sale of alcohol for general consumption was banned.

social drinker: An individual who drinks alcohol but does not have any problems associated with it, like losing control over how much is consumed.

withdrawal: A term used to describe the difficult and painful process an alcoholic goes through to reduce and ultimately eliminate all alcohol from his system.

Organizations to Contact

There are many resources available to anyone seeking information on any aspect of alcoholism. The fastest way to get information is to visit or telephone your school health counselor or a local mental health center. The following national organizations all provide informational pamphlets and will be happy to respond to your letter or phone call.

Al-Anon Family Group Headquarters, Inc.
P. O. Box 862, Midtown Station
New York, NY 10018-0862
(212) 302-7240

The Al-Anon Family Groups (including Alateen, specifically for teenagers) are a fellowship of relatives and friends of alcoholics who share their experience. The one purpose of the Al-Anon Family Groups is to help families and friends of alcoholics. There are no dues for membership.

Alcoholics Anonymous World Services (AA)
P. O. Box 459
Grand Central Station
New York, NY 10163
(212) 686-1100

Alcoholics Anonymous is an organization for individuals recovering from alcoholism. AA maintains that members can solve their common problem and help others achieve sobriety through a twelve-step program that includes sharing experiences with other recovering alcoholics. AA offers numerous publications.

American Council on Alcoholism, Inc.

Health Education Center
White Marsh Business Center
5024 Campbell Blvd., Suite H
Baltimore, MD 21236
(800) 527-5344

The American Council on Alcoholism is a nonprofit health organization that has been serving the public since 1953. The council stresses the importance of education in fighting alcohol problems and alcoholism and promotes school and health programs, and employee assistance programs, to further this purpose.

Children of Alcoholics Foundation, Inc.

P. O. Box 4185
Grand Central Station
New York, NY 10163-4185
(800) 359-COAF

The Children of Alcoholics Foundation provides free information and referrals to young and adult children of alcoholics and helps young people learn about family alcoholism and how to give and get assistance. The foundation publishes a brochure for young people entitled: "If you Think Your Parents Drink Too Much. . . ." It also runs a comprehensive alcohol education and prevention program called "The Images Within: A Child's View of Parental Alcoholism." Drawings made by children from alcoholic families are an important part of this program.

Students Against Driving Drunk (SADD)

P. O. Box 800
Marlboro, MA 01752
(508) 481-3568

SADD is a student organization which aims to increase youth awareness of alcohol abuse. It urges students to take action against drunk driving and other alcohol-related behavior. The organization has a speakers bureau and publishes a newletter, pamphlets, and books.

Suggestions for Further Reading

Louie Anderson, *Dear Dad: Letters From An Adult Child*. New York: Viking-Penguin, 1989.

Charles P. Cozic and Karin Swisher, eds., *Chemical Dependency: Opposing Viewpoints*. San Diego: Greenhaven Press, 1991.

Paul Dolmetsch and Gail Mauricette, eds., *Teens Talk About Alcohol and Alcoholism*. New York: Doubleday and Co., 1987.

Ross Fishman, *Alcohol and Alcoholism*. New York: Chelsea House Publishers, 1986.

Janet Grosshandler, *Coping with Alcohol Abuse*. New York: Rosen Publishing Group, 1990.

Herma Silverstein, *Alcoholism*. New York: Franklin Watts, 1990.

Works Consulted

E. L. Abel, *Fetal Alcohol Syndrome and Fetal Alcohol Effects*. New York: Plenum, 1984.

Alcohol Problems in Your Community: What You Can Do to Help. New York: New York State Council on Alcoholism, New York State Division of Alcoholism and Alcohol Abuse, 1990.

The Bottom Line on Alcohol in Society, vol. 12, no. 2. Alcohol Research Information Service, 1106 East Oakland Avenue, Lansing, MI 48906.

Sharon Wegscheider Cruse, *Another Chance: Hope and Health for the Alcoholic Family*, 2nd ed. Palo Alto, CA: Science and Behavior Books, 1989.

Armando Favazza, "Alcohol and Special Populations," *Journal of Studies on Alcohol*, Supplement No. IX, January 1981.

Herbert Fingarette, *Heavy Drinking: The Myth of Alcoholism as a Disease*. Berkeley: University of California Press, 1988.

Kathleen Whalen FitzGerald, *Alcohol: The Genetic Inheritance*. New York: Doubleday, 1988.

Boyd Gibbons, "Alcohol: The Legal Drug," *National Geographic*, February 1992.

Stanley E. Gitlow, M.D., "A Pharmacological Approach To Alcoholism," *AA Grapevine*, October 1968.

Daniel Goleman, "Family Rituals May Promote Better Emotional Adjustment," *The New York Times*, March 11, 1992.

Daniel Goleman, "Wisdom on Alcoholic's Child Called Stuff of Fortune Cookies," *The New York Times*, February 19, 1992.

Donald W. Goodwin, *Is Alcoholism Hereditary?* New York: Ballentine Books, 1988.

Sandie Johnson, "Recent Research: Alcohol and Women's Bodies," *Alcohol and Drugs Are Women's Issues, Volume One: A Review of the Issues*, Paula Roth, ed. Metuchen, NJ: Women's Action Alliance and Scarecrow Press, 1991.

Arthur Jones, "Another Japanese First: Death from Overwork," *National Catholic Reporter*, May 11, 1990.

M. P. Koss and M. R. Harvey, *The Rape Victim: Clinical and Community Approaches to Treatment*. Lexington, MA: Stephen Greene Press, 1987.

Robin A. LaDue, "Coyote Returns: Survival for Native American Women," *Alcohol and Drugs Are Women's Issues, Volume One: A Review of the Issues*, Paula Roth, ed. Metuchen, NJ: Women's Action Alliance and Scarecrow Press, 1991.

Phyllis A. Langton, *Drug Use and the Alcohol Dilemma*. Boston: Allyn and Bacon, 1991.

Mission Statement, Partnership for a Drug-Free America, 666 Third Avenue, New York, NY 10017; 1991.

The Most Frequently Asked Questions About Alcoholism, American Council on Alcoholism, Inc., Health Education Center, White Marsh Business Center, 5024 Campbell Blvd., Suite H, Baltimore, MD 21236; 1990.

Jack Mumey, *The Joy of Being Sober*. Chicago: Contemporary Books, 1984.

Edgar P. Nace, M.D., *The Treatment of Alcoholism*. New York: Brunner/Mazel Publishers, 1987.

"Native Americans Use Ancient Tribal Customs to Help Heal Modern Health Problems," *Advances*, 1991.

Stanton Peele, Ph.D., and Archie Brodsky, *The Truth About Addiction and Recovery*. New York: Simon and Schuster, 1991.

Karen S. Peterson, "Putting a Cap on Teenage Drinking," *USA Today*, May 15, 1990.

Paula Roth, ed., *Alcohol and Drugs Are Women's Issues, Volume One: A Review of the Issues*. Metuchen, NJ: Women's Action Alliance and Scarecrow Press, 1991.

Elizabeth A. Ryan, *Straight Talk About Drugs and Alcohol*. New York: Facts on File, 1989.

Eric Ryerson, *When Your Parent Drinks Too Much: A Book For Teenagers*. New York: Facts on File, 1985.

Secretary of Health and Human Services, *Seventh Special Report to the U.S. Congress on Alcohol and Health*. Rockville, MD: U.S. Department of Health and Human Services, 1990.

Boris M. Segal, *The Drunken Society: Alcohol Abuse and Alcoholism in the Soviet Union*. New York: Hippocrene Books, 1990.

George Steinmetz, "The Preventable Tragedy: Fetal Alcohol Syndrome," *National Geographic*, February 1992.

Jean Kennedy Tracy, "Living with an Alcoholic," *Alcohol and Drugs Are Women's Issues, Volume One: A Review of the Issues*, Paula Roth, ed. Metuchen, NJ: Women's Action Alliance and Scarecrow Press, 1991.

Understanding Ourselves and Alcoholism. New York: Al-Anon Family Groups, P.O. Box 862, Midtown Station, New York, NY 10018; 1990.

Dennis Wholey, *The Courage To Change*. Boston: Houghton Mifflin, 1984.

J. Winski, "Alcohol Warnings Favored," *Advertising Age*, April 9, 1990.

Index

About the Author

Arthur Diamond, born in Queens, New York, has lived and worked in Colorado, New Mexico, and Oregon. He received a bachelor's degree in English from the University of Oregon and a master's degree in English/Writing from Queens College.

Mr. Diamond is the author of several nonfiction books, including *The Bhopal Chemical Leak* and *Smallpox and the American Indian* in Lucent Books' World Disasters series. He lives in his boyhood home with his wife, Irina, and their children, Benjamin Thomas and Jessica Ann.

Picture Credits
